The Godfather

Business Lessons from the Godfather

by Dr. Michael Francis Tendler

GORGEOUS
FLOWER
COMBOS
PLANT ADVICE
LIFE
THE
ROCKET MAN
TITANIC
ELTON
JOHN
LIFE
50
YEARS
The
Godfather
The Story.
The Movies.
The Legacy.

DISCLAIMER:

By reading this document, you assume all risks associated with using the advice given below, with a full understanding that you, solely, are responsible for anything that may occur because of putting this information into action in any way, and regardless of your interpretation of the advice.

The content of this report is for educational purposes only. The information here is not intended to be nor should be misconstrued to be business advice or legal advice. While all care has been taken, it is the responsibility as the reader to ensure any activities he/she engages in follow to the applicable laws in his/her country, state, county and local area. No liability is accepted by the author or publisher for any damage caused from the information in this report. There are no guarantees spelled out within this report that the results contained within, are guaranteed in any way. By reading past this point you are accepting these terms and conditions.

[NO] Can Be Edited Completely
[NO] Can Claim
[NO] Cab be added to paid membership site
[NO] Can be packaged with other products
[NO] Can be sold
[NO] Can sell Resale Rights

The ideas, content and principles in this book are provided on an advisory basis only. Results of application are entirely dependent on the abilities of individual companies or individuals. Results may vary. No guarantee is made about earnings, financial or any other outcomes. Any and all forward looking statements are intended to express our opinion only of earnings potential. Many factors will be important in deciding your actual results and no guarantees are made that you will achieve any results from the ideas and techniques in this material. While all attempts have been made to verify information provided in this publication, neither the author nor the Publisher assumes any responsibility for errors, omissions or contrary interpretation of the subject matter. The Publisher also stresses that the information held here may be subject to varying state and/or local laws or regulations. All users are recommended to keep competent counsel to decide what state and / or local laws or regulations may apply to the user's particular business. The purchaser or reader of this publication assumes responsibility for the use of this information. Adherence to all applicable laws and regulations, both federal and state and local, governing professional licensing, business practices, advertising and all other aspects of doing business in the United States or any other jurisdiction is the responsibility of the purchaser or reader. The author and Publisher assume no responsibility or liability whatsoever on the behalf of any purchaser or reader of these materials. Every attempt is made to supply proper credit to the authors and owners of material quoted in this publication whenever possible. We do not claim ownership of any of their original works or products included in this publication. We do not claim ownership or copyright of or in any independent products mentioned or referred to in this publication. Nor do we intentionally infringe on anyone's copyrighted material.

Table of Contents

Acknowledgements

In business as in life, there are so many people to thank. I am sure I have omitted people that have my gratitude. After forty-five years, I have decided to come out of retirement being prodded by my friends and family tired of my ranting and complaining about today's businesspeople.

My heartfelt thanks

Jim Reed, who taught a street kid to be an executive

Melodee Kessler, she saved me from my demons

Peter Nauert, a friend who I miss dearly

Steve "Pucky" Weiss, no better friend in the world

Mercer Redcross, my lifelong friend who motivated me to begin again

And to my sons, I love you.

YouTube, Facebook, Instagram bombards the internet with software with "sure fire" marketing ploys, and online coaching before the business basics are in place. What happened to the understanding of a profit and loss statement, fixed cost verses variable costs, and GETTING A PAYCHECK WEEKLY…?

I will invite you for in-depth training at the end of my eBook or hard copy. I will make the offer for you to look deep into your business and end money worries with my,"5 Step Business Success System." It is time to get renewed and challenge ourselves to manage, plan and control our family businesses like the "Big Boys!"

This short eBook is meant to give your ideas from a father of a family-owned business to a son whose interests are like your own. It is not meant to be magic or a "quick fix" formula to ensure instant success or transform your company. It is intended to have you enjoy the 50th Anniversary of a classic motion picture with an insight into how their business relates to you and your family business.

As a side note, I refer to sales and salespeople as a business as well. I find salespeople generally do not consider themselves in this manner. My goal was to make this information fun and informative and reader friendly.

Mike Tendler

Business Lessons from The Godfather

Introduction

"The picture that almost wasn't."

The Godfather is one of the greatest movies of all time. Directed by Francis Ford Coppola on a $6 million budget, completed ahead of schedule, and was the first film in history to take in a million dollars a day. The film nominated for 11 Oscars, won three, and changed cinema forever. The studio "suits "hated everything about **The Godfather**. It was not until Michael Corleone (Al Pacino) put one in the head and throat of a police captain and the Turk and getting brains all over his Ivy League suit. It was that scene that cemented Coppola's argument to make the film.

Paramount studio execs did not like the actors, the director, the setting, the music, the theme nothing suited their vision of a "gangster" motion picture. The studio did not even like the puppet strings logo or the period and flash - back scenes. However, that was only the beginning of the problems.

Paramount promoted **The Godfather** as the Italian mob drama made by Italians. However, Italian Americans portrayed as criminals in the movies, increased their emotions and were upset. Ironically, the real-life Godfather, Joseph Colombo, of one of the five crime families, formed The Italian American Civil Rights League in 1969. Despite the other families warning against of such a move by attracting too much focus on the crime families. They demanded the words "mafia" and "Cosa Nostra" pulled from the script and that all the money the movie made at its premier donated to their fund to build a new hospital.

The Godfather producer Al Ruddy and Colombo had a "sit down" (a Mafia term for a high-level meeting at which time a decision will be forthcoming) at the Park Sheraton Hotel. Ruddy agreed and the term "Mafia" was removed from the script and Colombo gave his blessing. James Caan later got friendly with "made men" who frequented the set often during the filming.

Of course, every actor wanted the role of Don Vito Corleone. Marlon Brando cast after disagreements with the execs and Coppola stuck to his guns that Brando, despite his reputation for being difficult was the absolute perfect choice for the role. History shows, Brando tricked by Coppola into doing a screen test for Paramount president Stanley Jaffe. Brando stuck cotton balls in his cheeks, put shoe polish in his hair to darken it, and rolled his collar, and he wore a mouthpiece that a dentist made for him and spoke with a gruff voice.

The casting of Michael took a different twist. In the book, Michael is tall and blond. Paramount Pictures wanted Robert Redford or Ryan O'Neal to play the returning World War II vet and college graduate. Warren Beatty turned down the role, big mistake Warren. Pacino cemented the role in the wedding scene with Diane Keaton over a plate of pasta and Lucca Brasi mumbling in the wings.

The studio auditioned Caan, Martin Sheen, Dustin Hoffman, David Carradine, Dean Stockwell, and Robert De Niro, who also auditioned for Sonny. Coppola wanted theater actor Al Pacino but later saw him in the role of Michael. John Cazale got the part of Fredo Corleone. John Cassavetes and Peter Falk were both approached to play consigliere Tom Hagen.

Sonny Corleone originally awarded to Carmine Caridi. James Caan and Robert Duvall both acted in Coppola's earlier endeavors and won over his critics. The "trash can" seen was Caan's shinning scene and test for the part. Talia Shira played Connie Corleone is the sister of director Coppola.

Coppola constantly undermined during filming due to Paramount keeping a close eye on production costs. The studio thought that the film was *too talky and introspective* lacking action featured in GANSTER flicks. Paramount threatened Coppola with a "violence coach." The studio threatened to fire Coppola, Brando, and Pacino kept solidarity by threatening to quit if the director taken off the project. What a mess!

Note: The end results. ***The Godfather*** was the highest-grossing film of 1972. For a while, it was the highest-grossing film ever made. Pacino, Caan, and Robert Duvall were all nominated for Best Supporting Actor Oscars. Coppola nominated for Best Director. *Brando won the Oscar for Best Actor and refused the award.* Puzo and Coppola won the Best Adapted Screenplay Oscar. The movie won the Academy Awards for Best Picture. Paramount was happy. They released ***The Godfather Part II*** in 1974 and film analysts think that was an even better film. In fact, was the only sequel nominated for an Academy award. ***The Godfather Part III*** released in 1990 and, while it is far better than its reputation suggests and an utter disappointment.

Forward

I have watched **the Godfather** countless times and I am always amazed at the talent of the actors and the roles they played with perfection. The casting and scripting are certainly iconic. When you pause to think about the THEME and MESSAGING is remarkable. It dawned on me, the movie is a story of a father managing a family business and mentoring his sons as an *exit strategy*. The industry is unusual, but the principles are systematic as any business on Main Street.

Vito Corleone learned business the hard way. Formulating his philosophy took years to master. He was an example of business ethics, demeanor, and role model to his sons and crime family members. One sibling paid attention, Michael, his youngest. The least likely to be engaged in the family business.

I thoroughly enjoyed authoring this book by carefully absorbing The Don's teachings, mannerisms and applying them to everyday business and sales situations. By mastering these principles, you will enjoy a smooth sales process and defeat any objections before they occur. Vito and Michael in instances involving Sollozzo and Barvzini and later Hyman Roth and Moe Green used these principles.

I used various and recognizable phases and platitudes spoken by varies characters in the movie and added context as it relates to sales and business insights. I expounded and took the opportunity to add and use my own thoughts, experiences, and real-life examples to enhance the message of your reading. Hopefully, this will be helpful to you in your sales and business experience when preparing a presentation or content for a training program.

Things have changed in our world and our business environment! The patterns needed for success rarely change regardless of online sales or the face-to-face scenario. A presentation with poise and professionalism to secure a desired result is still the goal a …. sale!

I am mindful that we have sales and business habits we have developed over the years. We need to adjust the bad and improve on the good. Simply knowing what is wrong is one thing, correcting them is quite another. Ironically, I have seen through my years in sales management, consulting and business coaching people are slow to adjust even after the facts presented and proven. The fact is 20% of business fail in year one, 50% in year 5, 65% of small business fail in less than 10 years.

According to SCORE (Service Corps of Retired Executives), there are reasons businesses **fail:** lack of money, changes in the economy, ineffective management, employee turnover, theft, illness, or death of the owner, #1 cause, lack of business basics!

This book, however, intended to shed light on the WISDOM of Vito and Michael and to enjoy the scenes from the Godfather. Enjoy and learn from the lessons of a father- to- son running a "family business."

Keep in mind, all business started out like yours, a family business and from less than perfect conditions.

- ➢ Walmart (Sam worked for JC Penny),
- ➢ Starbucks (Schultz rejected 242 times seeking capital)
- ➢ Mac Donald's (Ray Kruk refinanced his home)
- ➢ Motown (Berry Gordy borrowed $900 from his family)
- ➢ Mary Kay (started with her life savings $5,000)
- ➢ Microsoft (Bill Gates started in a garage),

- ➢ Berkshire Hathaway (started at $11.375 a share)
- ➢ Ford Motors (Henry was a machinist one of eight children)
- ➢ NIKE (Phil Knight wrote a college paper on making shoes in Japan)
- ➢ Go Daddy (Bob Parsons an ex-Marine worked in a steel mill)
- ➢ Onassis Shipping (Onassis began as a switchboard operator)
- ➢ Charles Schwab (claimed bankruptcy)
- ➢ Mattel (began selling picture frames)
- ➢ Amazon (Bezos began in his kitchen)
- ➢ KFC (The Colonel was an insurance salesperson)
- ➢ Wrigley's (Bill Wrigley was a soap salesperson)
- ➢ Harley Davidson (was a bicycle company)
- ➢ Dollar General (Cal Turner expanded his father's retail business)
- ➢ ACE Hardware (two Chicago guys merged and named it after ACE fighter pilots)

Ok, let us begin and have fun, "Sales Lessons from the Godfather"

Mike Tendler

Lesson #1

"I'll make him an offer he can't refuse!"

The iconic scene when Don Vito assures his Godson, Johnny Fontane that movie produce Waltz will give him the role in the upcoming picture. Arguably one of the most memorable scenes ever in Hollywood.

Let us analyze this scene and observe how we can learn a valuable lesson in our business and sales presentations. What was the offer? The **OFFER** needs to get the listeners attention at once and creates CURIOSITY and leads to a conversation. Tom Hagen walks in unannounced and approaches Waltz. Hagen starts with an introduction by saying he was sent by a friend of Johnny Fontane's. "Waltz is listening" was his immediate response.

An offer needs to suggest that there is a ROI attached. The RETURN ON INVESTMENT is a means of saving money, time and of course, "What's in it for me?" **The offer needs an Action opening!**

Tom Hagen approached Waltz and made an ACTION OPENING INTO AN OFFER. .... **Action opening** ... *"You have a star going from marihuana to heroine and there are union issues.... **OFFER,** "We can make go away just give Johnny a part in your picture."*

Tom's mission is to set an appointment. One goal, get the appointment.

At dinner later that evening Waltz got angry and rejected the offer. The entire sequence was pre-planned by Vito expecting Waltz's reaction. Of course, we know what happened next. A game of horseshoes anyone?

In sales, the more curious the prospect becomes it is easier to add value and solutions that will lead to a profitable ending. Asking the right questions will tell us what the *client wants and what we can offer to solve for X.* Once proven, we need to get agreement that our **OFFER** is the solution.

Our goal is to "find out what the client wants and is willing to pay for!" We accomplish this by creating interest that leads to a conversation that I refer to as the "**interview**" stage. **Asking questions that we know the answers to is learned behavior!** The days of those "canned" phrases or trial close irritating the client are over. The ABC sales technique is annoying and wrong! We look to have "affirmations" that we found the solution by eliminating risk the consumer sees as a fatal mistake in the decision-making process…." seek and thou shall find!"

Health Insurance

Ms. Jones, I am Mike Smith with the Star Health Insurance Agency the leading agency in our region. I see on your inquiry (lead) you have two underage children… Tell me is a zero deductible for doctors' visits for those runny noses and untimely colds and fevers important to you? Response … Yes of course.

Tell me, are you aware of the plan offered exclusively for families with young children by my company in your county? …

Back to school is approaching. Do you want to avoid those runny noses and sniffles?

Budget is always a concern. I bet you are no different.

Affordable does not have to be sacrificing benefits.

Are you aware we don't have a "one suit fits all" approach?

Ms. Jones, do you see the benefit of spending 20 minutes with me to discuss the plans available and see those zero deductibles in action! … … YOUR ON!

Social Media Marketing

Mr. Jones, I am Mike Jones with Muti Media Marketing the foremost lead generation company in our region.

Why do some companies attract buyers, and some don't? Budget is always a concern. I am sure your no different.

Do you feel your system can manage all the leads we generate?

Do you prefer emailing or calling our quality leads?

We tend to generate activity quickly. Is that ok or do you need more time?

Our clients thought that social media marketing is too expensive and technical, but it does not have to be if you follow our simple system. A quick overview of our system will put you at ease and together we can get those buyers in your door?. YOUR ON!

Car Warranty

Mr./Ms. Jones I am Mike Smith with warranty company you have heard about on TV. You contacted us for a reason.

I 'm sure you have seen the prices of new and used cars these days? That makes our existing car like gold, doesn't it?

What would the consequences be if it were to need expensive repairs?

What would being $3.000 out of pocket that mean to our family?

I am sure you reviewed you auto coverage and found repairs are questionable.

Let us put our heads together on an affordable way to prevent this **when it happens** and spend 10 minutes to review your options… ….YOUR ON!

Life Insurance

Are you aware Wall Street people make money even when you lose yours?

if you are lucky to make money guess what, it is taxable.

Mr./Ms. There is a way to save money with no risk and NO TAX….!

Do you have an IRA? Do you wish you did?

Not having WORKERS COMP is unfair to the self- employed. I have a solution.

Did you know you can function as if you were your own bank?

Would you like me to help you develop "A no worry plan?" It is easier than you think. One of my favorites.

By spending 20 minutes together I can reveal the information they don't want you to know. I CAN END YOUR MONEY WORRIES FORVER.

Please join me online at my web site ….

From here you can begin a conversation or **an interview** and find out exactly, "What the prospect wants?" Once that is FIRMELY established, then getting an AGREEMENT that you are the person and company that they want to do business with and your plan, product or service is their solution. Your ability to use **Specialized Knowledge**, commonly referred to as Product Knowledge here is crucial whether online or face to face. Your ability to call upon your working knowledge of your product, service, or plan to solve problems is what they are after. Expressing the differentiation from our competition needs to be at our fingertips!

We need to focus our efforts on developing a positive questioning model that replaces the old way of doing things. Arousing the prospects CURIOSITY with an ACTION OPENING being beware not to come off too **"salesy"** in the opening. It is important to take a leadership role.

I teach something different than any coach or trainer. I refer to it as the **"INSTITUTIONAL."** After the interview stage, now it is the perfect time to talk about us!

Mr./MS Jones, I know a lot about you allow me to tell you about myself and **my company**. We are proud of our _________ years in business and our customer service that stands the test of time. We differ from other companies because we! Our price and quality guarantees are first in our industry, and we are open _________ per week/year just in case you need us.

Sales professionals neglect talking proudly about their company. This can be a HUGH mistake! The customer will be dealing with your service dept, accounting, customer service and so on.

Remember Tom with Waltz? An ACTION OPEN got his attention, didn't it?

Let us review what we learned:

1. A clear but brief introduction
2. An '**Action opening**" that creates curiosity ending in a conversation
3. Present a well-focused **OFFER**
4. Set a time for an appointment **The Interview Stage** Asking questions supply solutions **by** presenting our product, plan, or service
5. The Institutional

I go into this is detail in my live seminars / webinars and coaching sessions!

Lesson #2

"Don Corleone, I need a man who has powerful friends. I need a million dollars in cash. I need, Don Corleone, with those politicians you carry in your pocket, like so many nickels and dimes."
Virgil Sollozzo

Sollozzo was a patient and methodical man and was also extremely cunning and intelligent. He saw the future in drug trafficking, but he needed to have a powerful ally. What was he looking for? Obviously, a PARTNERSHIP! He has the muscle and production capability; he looks for capital and political protection. This a valuable lesson learned in our business practices today. Here is a real-life example.

Before Obama Care, I saw the possibility of selling health insurance online. At that time, all sales where "face to face" or" belly to belly" was the vernacular at that time. People in the industry thought I needed psychiatric help. I sent almost one year looking for a PARTNER that needed what I could offer; a trained field staff in return for the software to make my vision a reality. I eventually found the Continental General with a software program not used to its fullest. A bright CEO who bought into my vision and a I hit it off immediately.

We created the first online health insurance company. I needed one more piece to complete the circle. Our sales increased very quickly after one more PARTNERSHIP created. Remember, there was no **Zoom** at that time. An insurance salesperson created a **web- conference tool** that allowed the consumer to join us online at our web site. Our software designs the plan, the consumer signs the doc's electronically, and we send it to be underwriting all in one step. Today this seems rudimentary, not so 20 years ago.

Let us be realistic and open minded to seeking PARTNERSHIPS where they might exist. The concept of working together and the value of "interdependency "is the result of advanced technology, diversified marketing strategies and our younger generation stepping up with creative ideas we need to embrace. I have always enjoyed PARTNERING with others on projects and over the years. I have learned what works and what does not. Here are my strategies that I use to help me build collaborative relationships.

Be Clear On What You Need To Accomplish

Being clear on what you would like to accomplish. The opportunity for you to seek out the right resources and partners who can help you achieve this. Ensure that these partners aligned with your values or else a cultural mismatch could ensue which will surely be very costly later. Be sure that you have a meaningful and workable product or service that is a "no brainer" to offer as a means for a PARTNERSHIP. A marketing partner needs a product, a sales staff needs a technology partner, a reliable shipping department needs a fulfillment system and is a real winner in finding a partner.

A bona fide accounting, legal and internal commission department accompanied with a sales staff offers endless opportunities for a successful partnership.

Be Open To Opportunities

When people collaborate, a new energy created is bigger than the sum of the parts. Innovative ideas flow which can result in projects bigger than you saw as possible. Why not outsource, or simply hire a marketing company? I bet, you tried that with only frustration and with little result for the money and time spent. Managing "outsource" partners is a topic I address in my workshops and webinars.

Hired to be a marketing consultant for a L.E.D. LIGHTING COMPANY that offered a remarkable product. They engineered and shipped the product from China. I saw to get traction, but the shipping department needed help in coordinating the process with China. A sales staff was imperative to call on distributors and demonstrate the amazing qualities of the product.

They tried outsourcing sales to a call center with little or no success. They tried an internal sales staff but the IRS issue of an employee or a 1099 independent contractor was becoming a headache with accounting. The software was not communicating with China to my liking. I proposed a solution.

I discovered a competitor was desperately trying to replicate our product with China. This notion was destined to end in court for sure and it did not need a rocket to see it. They had a sales staff and were well capitalized. I approached them with a proposed solution a COLLABORATION / PARTNERSHIP You have the sales staff and management; we have the ready-made product and shipping department. Looks like a match what do You think? After negotiating, the deal agreed upon and there were adjustments involving the staff on both sides. The communication at first was rocky, but level heads prevailed. I created a sales scripts and online website presentations and the business thrived.

Be Clear On Your Roles And Responsibilities

Knowing what you are committing to in the collaboration is key. Work to your strengths and have clear action plans so everyone knows what the goal is and a realistic period. Recognize that others work in diverse ways and be flexible to accommodate others working practices. There will be bumps in the road but keep the communication lines open. Having ongoing meetings and enjoining the staff members is imperative. The PARNERSHIP / COLLABERATION is as important to the team on both sides so get them involved.

A clear chart of JOB DESCRIPTIONS and communication lines needs to be addressed at the very start of the relationship. Too often, the business owner neglects this business practice and not doing so will come back to bite you. Go online and get a free job description template and begin the process. *The partners especially need to be specific and realistic on their roles as well.*

The entire team needs to express their feelings, doubts, and concerns. This will prove to be is healthy in any relationship and collaborative relationships are no different. Each party must feel able to say what is on their mind.

Listen carefully to what your **collaborative partner does not say!** This is where you might find the real gold in your conversations. Be sure to get the grievances out in the open quickly because delays will tent to fester and linger if not dealt with urgency. Do not allow grip sessions to be the norm in the organization look to inspire solutions. Remember, the end game is in **profits** and moving the company forward.

Lay Out The Ground Rules

Having clarity over the ground rules such as time spent, and money commitments is paramount. These issues need to be upfront or else it creates animosity at a later stage. Confusion appears around how profits get divided. Choice varies from profits earned funneled back in the business or pocket the cash. This area is where caution begins.

The most important thing is that that the partners agree upfront. Never assume that because you are collaborating everything is shared 50:50!!!

REMEMBER, all businesses are family businesses and spouses informed of these disscisions as well.

The allocation of profits is a function involving all the partners, bookkeepers, and accountants at your disposal. Do we sock away the money? Do we pay off debts? Do we hire young MBAs to improve our systems? Do we seek more marketing help? Obviously, the need for a "meeting of the minds" is crucial. The result needs to be clear and agreed upon. Do not leave the table until RESOLVED!

Being able to express your feelings, doubts and concerns is healthy in any relationship and collaborative relationships are no different. Each party must feel able to say what is on their mind. Always listen carefully to what your collaborative partner AND AGAIN, "Listen carefully to what your **collaborative partner doesn't say**!" especially when the conversation revolves around money.

There are many collaborative opportunities out there so please make sure you choose a collaborative partner that you like and can BENEFIT EQUALLY. The energy dynamic needs to be positive and engaging to attract clients. Typically, we are engaging in collaboration to use resources and so make work more effortless. Find reasons to celebrate small victories often with rewards and remember plaques are nice… …MONEY IS NICER! Do not sweat the small stuff!

Lesson #3

Rarely do we see the Don as angered as he was with Santino by interrupting his train of thought with Sollozzo and his proposal. "Santino, come here, what is the matter with you…. never tell anyone outside the family what you are thinking again!" He made his point clear. *Notice however, everyone has left the room BEFORE the Don let him have it.* This point in the scene is we all have learned "**Praise in public but criticize in private**" for a reason?

Most managers have heard the phrase, "**Praise in public; criticize in private.**" It simply means that when you have something positive to say about a team member, make sure others are aware of the praise, but if you are issuing a correction or reprimand, manage it one-on-one. It is a long-standing mantra in management circles. Nothing gained by a PUBLIC flogging which only disrupts moral and lingers as gossip in the break room. Praise heightens the message on what is at the company's values. Nothing gained with public criticism and a teaching moment lost. However, that is the secondary message in this scene.

Listening is THE **most important aspect of sales**. The more you can gather about your prospect the more likely you will make the sale. I do not just mean listening to the words your prospect says but also to the tone of voice, their reactions and energy. Too often, not listening this is the most common mistake repeated over and over.

When you realize that your voice is the loudest voice in the room, I promise, you are not actively listening. To make matters worse, when your inner voice is overpowering when someone else is speaking, you cannot be in FACT FINDING mode. In fact, it might just put you in ASSUMPTION MODE and I will bet that you are, "Thinking what you are about to say and missing what the prospct is telling you!" It is critically important for salespeople and sales leaders and business owners to control their own emotions and head talk. Without that control, you miss both content and context in a conversation.

Active listening is also about patience. Listeners should not interrupt with questions or comments. Active listening involves giving the other person time to explore their thoughts and feelings. As you cultivate the habit of listening sincerely, *you invite people to open up.* They can sense when you will not be jumping to conclusions based on superficial details. They also realize when you care enough about them to listen attentively.

Active listening in your business conversations allows you to uncover information that your competition may not get and that you might never hear when passively listening. It takes practice and humility to become effective at active listening. When I work with sales teams, I challenge them after the ACTION OPENING STAGE to engage in the INTERIEW STAGE. That stage of the conversation requires intense listening. The active listening button should always be on. In sales or in negotiations removing ambiguity means that *you are in seek-to-understand mode as opposed to seek-to-reply to mode.*

Hearing is an accidental and automatic brain response to sound that requires no effort. Listening, on the other hand, is purposeful and focused rather than accidental. As a result, it requires motivation and effort. Effective listeners make sure to let others know that they have been heard and encourage them to share their thoughts and feelings fully.

Sollozzo paid attention as an ACTIVE LISTENER to Santino's outburst and removed all ambiguity all right! Sonny's out burse almost got the Don assassinated. "Sonny was hot for my deal" he commented to Tom assuming the Don was dead. Sollozzo believed once the Don was out of the way he could re-negotiate with Santino. For our purposes," What happens in the board room, stays in the board room!"

Lesson #4

"You're getting a real reputation Sonny; I hope you are enjoying it?"

Sonny was the oldest, most impulsive, and violent of Vito's sons. Before Michael's rise to power was the most involved in the Corleone crime family. It was Sonny, who was supposed to head the family business after the death of the Don. His devotion to his father earned his nickname, Sonny. He attacked Michael after deciding to tell their father that he had enlisted in the Marines and dropped out of college on their father's birthday in 1941. Sonny believed that people who fought in the military were "saps" because they risk their lives for strangers, and that "Your country ain't your blood." This was meet with varying opinions at the dinner table and Fredo condoned Michael's decision.

Sonny's famous temper was a reputation well known in the underworld circles and later the cause of his brutal murder. *Reputation* comes from the Latin word *reputationem,* which means "consideration." It is how people consider, or label, you — good or bad. The noun *reputation* can also mean "being known for having a specific skill or characteristic." For example, if you have a reputation for being late, or unprepared, opinionated, or conceded or in Sonny's case, easy to raise to violence. This considered as a personality trait or defining characteristic. Good or bad, you own it!

You reputation was create as early as childhood i.e., Little Jonny is a sound sleeper, Suzy is a good eater, Little Bobbie is always cheerful, Mary is cranky when she wakes up, Alex is big for his age, Salley is the smartest in her class. A widespread belief that someone or something has a particular habit or characteristic can begin that early in life. Reputations worry everyone from time to time especially when you are in school at work or with family members.

The Don has a reputation of being respectful, family orientated, powerful, deliberate, not greedy, modest, a man of his word, and a man of reason. A lengthy list of favorable traits created over a lifetime. The other Don's had reputations as well however, not so favorable. Tattaglia considered a pimp, low class and uses his family to carryout murder while Barzani although cunning, was known as violent and ruthless. Reputations well deserved.

The uncomfortable truth is *we do not always come across the way we intend.* We cannot see ourselves truly objectively, and neither can anyone else. Human beings have a strong tendency to distort other people's feedback to fit their own views. Life is simply easier and more rewarding when people as they say, "get you."

There is nothing employees hate more than a boss with a negative reputation. They send as much time with you as their own families and expect their time and effort to be rewarding. In any company, there are bound to be employees from distinct cultures, backgrounds, and personalities. Of course, every person should be hired based on their skills. A good boss also makes sure that all employees abide by company rules and regulation by doing their duties effectively and grow professionally and personally and use their skills to help the entity.

Based on universities studies, the single most valued quality is INTEGRITY in their boss's business life and personal life. Your attitude and outward behavior towards your spouse by your staff and employees noticed and evacuated. A leader with integrity gives the workers a sense of security and assurance that their boss will look out for what is best for them and their careers. A good boss/ leader should have both integrity and honesty in the office and at home. Is it possible to have integrity in business and be not so honest in our personal life?

The four ways to change your reputations and start today.

1. Think about why you want to change your reputation.
Be honest with yourself and figure out why you really want to change in your business life and personal life. Look for professional, spiritual help and family support. Again, all business is a family business and need to be involved.

2. Develop a "profile" of the ideal you.
Write a description of the new you that is realistic and keep it in front of you daily. The auto biography of Ben Franklin is a perfect place to start.

3. Make a realistic, detailed, and specific plan to change your reputation.
Nothing can change or improve without a specific period to monitor results. Set goals correctly. Set goals that are achievable and measurable. Use the SMART method when setting goals.

4. Celebrate" small successes."
"**Success** is a series of **small** wins" Recognizing and **celebrating small** successes boosts your self-esteem as well at it should. Give yourself a "High five!"

Lesson #5

*"Alfredo, you are my brother and i love you
but don't take sides with anyone against the family again!"*

In this scene, he Corleone family has eyes on moving their operations to Las Vegas. Moe Green stands in their way due to his partnership in the Vegas casino. Michael has other ideas as he enters the lavage room where the meeting was held. He offers (threatens) to" buy-out" Green when Brother Alfredo makes a major mistake in interrupting Michael in Green's presence.

Fredo was clumsy, uncoordinated and could not be confident. He paled in comparison to his brothers and needed reassurance. The type of reassurance that comes from a father. Vito could have taught his middle son to be more confident and assertive, but Fredo was too busy trying to keep the lifestyle that he was getting accustomed. Michael was aware of his short comings and was ready to accept them knowing his duties in the casino were "token" at best. He was still a Corleone! Therefore, all loyalties pledged to the family with no exception.

When Green baulked at the offer by Michael of the buy-out and stomped, yelled, and ranted. Green also accused of slapping Fredo in public, Michael let his feelings be known on behave of his sibling.

It was at that juncture, Fredo appeared to side with Green and thus the famous line. Was Michael at fault in this situation?

What can we learn from this scene? Did Michael assume Fredo was informed on his intention to spring the news on Green? Obviously not! Fredo acted badly, not informed ahead of time was a mistake. Fredo instinctively referred to Tom to step in and talk to the "Don." The message being, the Don (Vito) would have managed the situation and informed Fredo before the arrival of Michael.

I have extraordinarily strong feelings on this topic. From years of experience in corporate America. I have seen this play out too many times. Insurance agents taking sides against underwriters, underwriters taking sides against sales, sales taking sides against shipping, shipping taking side against manufacturers, assembly taking sides against engineering. Ironically, they are all on the same team or family.

This shows a complete lack of communication with your company team members. Does anyone really see any value in "disrespecting your company "and believing this will show favor with our customer? Of course not! So, way allow it to continue?

Disrespect in the workplace can creep in whenever there is a lack of **transparency.** Lack of **transparency** means that the team does not see the need to fill in the blanks. The lack of access to information about the organization's progress, and results, not clearly presented leads to misunderstandings loss of faith in company values and competency. Be clear about what is going on in the business and keep everyone on the team informed and on the same page. The department heads need to disclose all the issues, good and bad, and put them on the table to enable a positive resolve and understanding in every aspect of our business.

I was ridiculed for allowing my managers to be witness of all our corporate financials and insisted they managed to the bottom line and share their successes as well as their failures. I got this idea from Jack Welsh of GE fame. "Face reality as it is, not as it was or as you wish it to be.", a favorite quote from Jack. Many times, I'm completely wrong, but all you do is back up and start over."

An example, "Never taking sides against the family." A young hire as a mortgage loan officer came into my office railing about a value place on a property by our star appraiser. The property was offered by his real estate broker that was undoubtably his best client. As a rookie he had no right to take sides against our appraiser and I went, "Off the deep end." I blasted him so loudly the office stopped and came to a dead silence. To this day I regret my outburst, and this young man and I often laugh about it and review my bad behavior. The message, the appraiser is on our team to protect us from over valuing a property we are lending on and "never take sides against the family!" My approach was off base.

> Loyalty demands that you have created a workplace culture where your employees like to collaborate and share ideas. Be supportive and keep up to date on Company news and announcement. Employees NEVER suffer from information overload when it comes to the health and wellbeing of their company.

> Employers are responsible for keeping employees informed about substance-specific requirements and which need immediate attention TO PROMOTE STABILITY.

> Encourage employees to communicate with you and each other when they have questions, or they are unsure about situations, or just want to clarify something.

> Whether it is daily, weekly, bi-weekly, monthly, or quarterly, meetings are valuable tools for supplying the latest news and developments within the company. Having regular scheduled meetings allow those from different departments to know what is going on in the greater landscape of the business.

> Show progress! Everyone loves to hear that his or her arduous work is paying off. Give your employees feedback on how they and the company are performing.

Epilogue

imply a series of simplified techniques to digest, but not intended to be a cure-all to all the sales and business issues in our daily lives. Reading is not enough. I offered ideas and methods that should be followed up on by using the Godfather as a fun way of looking at a "family business." I hope we meet in person, and I can further teach my, "Sales Success System" that helped so many in the past.

I would like to make a point that I always preach in my sessions and webinars. Never count on your presumed **sales ability**! It is always better to count on the understanding of the **CUSTOMERS BUYING MOTIVES**. Learn them by listening and address them one bite at a time and the sale will be yours for the asking.

One other thing, **PREPERATION!**

In an interview, the late Sammy Davis Jr. said something I always remembered. He said," When I walked on stage, regardless of in a small café or a theater the size of a football field I give every performance as if it my last! I give the paying customer what they deserve, my absolute best!"

That same quality that Michael Jordon, Tom Brady, Michael Bubble' and Clive Davis have. It is the desire to be the best and their passion that separates them from their competitors. It is a derivative of faith and principles which ignites a sense of invincibility that they can call upon. Their abilities they achieved *by repetition.*

I enjoy watching the YOU TUBE CHANNEL and the Stanford Business School interviews with business leaders. This one evening, I noticed a video involving Floyd Mayweather and his Father Floyd Sr. In the locker room, getting ready for the bout. Senior was holding Floyd's well bandaged fists in both hands. Senior, starring at him directly, was going over all the possibilities his opponent would use to defeat him. Watch out for his left, his jab, move around counterclockwise and so on!

Floyd respectfully silent, listened and did not patronize his father. He stood up and shadow boxed in place warming up for a moment and said, "Dad, just another day in the gym!" The opponent, he is about to meet is also trained and skilled. Floyd was calm. Hs rigorous preparation in the gym, outlined by his father, prepared him for anything his opponent would use against him.

Reminiscent of the Mayweather encounter, the garden scene In the Godfather between son Michael and the elderly Don. Michael slouched over a lounge chair was being lectured. "Make sure all incoming phone calls are checked, the person who comes forward with the meeting is the "traitor" and you will be assassinated", he warned. "Men cannot be careless!" "I can handle it. I told you I can handle it!" Why was Michael so confident and calm? Preparation by repetition and carefully planning for any outcome ensures confidence and the ability to manage "details" and have instant "recall' powers.

I use the term, "recall powers" to illustrate once **specialized knowledge** becomes second nature it can be called upon in any situation. In the Mayweather example, the gym workouts drummed into his internal *motor memory* or Michael recalling the Don's constant reminding him to beware of *"careless" behaviors* are functions of "instant recall." Once mastered, your confidence will have your respond with a core of behaviors that become second nature resulting in your prospects problems being answered.

In the business world, SPECIALIZED KNOWLEDGE is the ability to use and call upon (instant recall) our knowledge of our plans or products to solve problems. The practical application of this body of knowledge allows us to differentiate our plan and products from our competition and convinces the customer/client we are the company and individual they want to do business with is the goal. This ability can only be achieved form repetition.

It has been a privilege to share my ideas and BUSINESS LESSONS FOR THE GODFATHER. I sure you realize there are no shortcuts to success only challenges. These simple but practical concepts are a good start. They can change the whole completion of your business and your approach to managing, planning, and controlling your enterprise.

By now you have come to realize, I use sales as a business as well. The face is salespeople do not consider themselves as a business enterprise which is a common mistake. The principles of business formation i.e., sole proprietor, S corp. verses C corp., accounting procedures, prospecting and marketing, funding and credit lines all need to be part of the sales business.

I teach the fundamentals to business as well as the salespersons in my 5 Step Business Success System. Please, don't hesitate to call me. I promise I will take every call and will do my best to answer all your questions. My promise to you!

1. Play the percentage
2. How The Rich Get Richer,
3. The Ultimate Success Tool
4. $500 Marketing Success Team
5. Manage, Plan and Control.

About the Author

Mike Tendler

Speaker, Author, and Motivator

Mike was born in Philadelphia, Pennsylvania. His competitive spirit and basketball talents made him a playground and schoolyard legend, which led as a top draft pick to play Professional Basketball representing Israel.

Upon his return to the States, Mike found his second calling as a top salesman and negotiator. He joined a prominent actuarial firm, where he was quickly promoted to V.P. of life insurance carrier acquisitions at a young age. He later excelled as an Executive Analyst with an international consulting firm specializing in helping small businesses reach their profitability.

Mike's financial abilities and business background and sales ability made him a natural to find his entrepreneurial spirit Mike soon broke all sales records when he created the first totally online Health Insurance Company. Mike was recognized as a visionary and a futurist in sales and marketing. The Self-Employed Insurance Group was created for the sale of health insurance. Mastering PAY PER CLICK internet and email advertising he designed and marketed his creation in forty-three states.

Today, Mike. Had come out of retirement to support small business's gain profitability by going back to basics.

Mike has been quoted in the Wall Street Journal, USA Today, hosted his own radio show, authored the "Sales Success System" and spoke at conventions and conferences throughout the country and has numerous certifications for financial and insurance advisors and was a million-dollar producer in health insurance and life and annuities. He is a certified Ramsey Financial Advisor.

Mike can be reached
717-853-3300
michaelftendler@gmail.com

www.ingramcontent.com/pod-product-compliance
Lightning Source LLC
Chambersburg PA
CBHW060925130726
48001CB00006B/2421